DATE DUE 2/02

GAYLORD			PRINTED IN U.S.A.

SandCastle 2

Homophones

We Have a Wee Whale

Amanda Rondeau

Publishing Company

JACKSON COUNTY LIBRARY SERVICES
MEDFORD, OREGON 97501

Published by SandCastle™, an imprint of ABDO Publishing Company, 4940 Viking Drive, Edina, Minnesota 55435.
Copyright © 2002 by Abdo Consulting Group, Inc. International copyrights reserved in all countries. No part of this book may be reproduced in any form without written permission from the publisher. SandCastle™ is a trademark and logo of ABDO Publishing Company. Printed in the United States.
Cover and interior photo credits: Comstock, Digital Vision, Eyewire Images, PhotoDisc

Library of Congress Cataloging-in-Publication Data

Rondeau, Amanda, 1974-
  We have a wee whale / Amanda Rondeau.
    p. cm. -- (Homophones)
  Includes index.
  Summary: Photographs and simple text introduce homophones, words that sound alike but are spelled differently and have different meanings.
  ISBN 1-57765-779-9
  1. English language--Homonyms--Juvenile literature. [1. English language--Homonyms.] I. Title. II. Series.

PE1595 .R74 2002
428.1--dc21
                                                2001053311

The SandCastle concept, content, and reading method have been reviewed and approved by a national advisory board including literacy specialists, librarians, elementary school teachers, early childhood education professionals, and parents.

Let Us Know

After reading the book, SandCastle would like you to tell us your stories about reading. What is your favorite page? Was there something hard that you needed help with? Share the ups and downs of learning to read. We want to hear from you! To get posted on the ABDO Publishing Company Web site, send us email at:

sandcastle@abdopub.com

About SandCastle™

Nonfiction books for the beginning reader

- Basic concepts of phonics are incorporated with integrated language methods of reading instruction. Most words are short, and phrases, letter sounds, and word sounds are repeated.

- Book levels are based on the ATOS™ for Books formula. Other considerations for readability include the number of words in each sentence, the number of characters in each word, and word lists based on curriculum frameworks.

- Full-color photography reinforces word meanings and concepts.

- "Words I Can Read" list at the end of each book teaches basic elements of grammar, helps the reader recognize the words in the text, and builds vocabulary.

- Reading levels are indicated by the number of flags on the castle.

SandCastle uses the following definitions for this series:

- Homographs: words that are spelled the same but sound different and have different meanings. *Easy memory tip: "-graph"= same look*

- Homonyms: words that are spelled and sound the same but have different meanings. *Easy memory tip: "-nym"= same name*

- Homophones: words that sound alike but are spelled differently and have different meanings. *Easy memory tip: "-phone"= sound alike*

Look for more SandCastle books in these three reading levels:

Level 1 (one flag)	**Level 2** (two flags)	**Level 3** (three flags)

Grades Pre-K to K 5 or fewer words per page	**Grades K to 1** 5 to 10 words per page	**Grades 1 to 2** 10 to 15 words per page

Note: Some pages in this book contain more than 10 words in order to more clearly convey the concept of the book.

walk   wok

Homophones are words that sound alike but are spelled differently and have different meanings.

Ellen has to wait for her dad to finish.

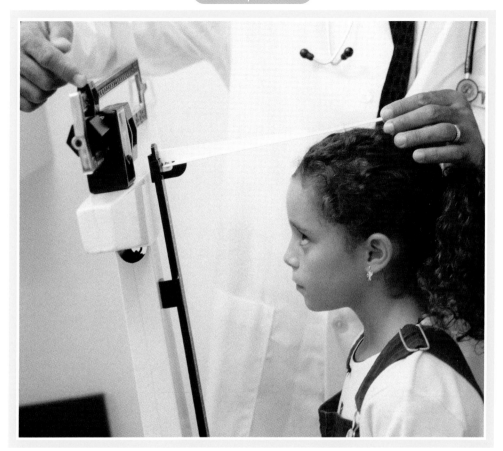

The doctor checks my height and weight.

The whale is under water.

Mika lets out a wail.

She is sad.

Amber is learning the way to care for flowers.

Eric and Jon weigh fruit at the store.

We like to wade in the water.

The large apples weighed a lot.

Julia can keep the hoops
around her waist.

Our parents tell us not to
waste food.

Mom goes to work five days a week.

Roberto and Mike are
not weak.
They carry the couch.

A mostly clear sky means good weather.

I wonder whether anyone is home.

I would like to play tennis.

What is the fence made of?

(wood)

Words I Can Read

Nouns

A noun is a person, place, or thing

couch (KOUCH) p. 17
dad (DAD) p. 6
doctor (DOK-tur) p. 7
fence (FENSS) p. 21
food (FOOD) p. 15
fruit (FROOT) p. 11
height (HITE) p. 7

sky (SKYE) p. 18
store (STOR) p. 11
tennis (TEN-iss) p. 20
wail (WALE) p. 9
waist (WAYST) p. 14
water (WAW-tur)
   pp. 8, 12
way (WAY) p. 10

weather (WETH-ur)
   p. 18
week (WEEK) p. 16
weight (WATE) p. 7
whale (WALE) p. 8
wok (WOK) p. 4
wood (WUD) p. 21
work (WURK) p. 16

Plural Nouns

A plural noun is more than one
person, place, or thing

apples (AP-uhlz)
   p. 13
days (DAYZ) p. 16
flowers (FLOU-urz)
   p. 10

homophones
   (HOME-uh-fonez)
   p. 5
hoops (HOOPZ) p. 14

meanings
   (MEE-ningz) p. 5
parents (PAIR-uhntz)
   p. 15
words (WURDZ) p. 5

Proper Nouns

A proper noun is the name of a person, place, or thing

Amber (AM-bur) p. 10

Ellen (EL-en) p. 6

Eric (ER-ik) p. 11

Jon (JON) p. 11

Julia (JOO-lee-uh) p. 14

Mika (MEE-kuh) p. 9

Mike (MIKE) p. 17

Mom (MOM) p. 16

Roberto (ROH-ber-toh) p. 17

Verbs

A verb is an action or being word

are (AR) pp. 5, 17

can (KAN) p. 14

care (KAIR) p. 10

carry (KA-ree) p. 17

checks (CHEKSS) p. 7

finish (FIN-ish) p. 6

goes (GOHZ) p. 16

has (HAZ) p. 6

have (HAV) p. 5

is (IZ) pp. 8, 9, 10, 19, 21

keep (KEEP) p. 14

learning (LURN-ing) p. 10

lets (LETSS) p. 9

like (LIKE) pp. 12, 20

made (MAYD) p. 21

means (MEENZ) p. 18

play (PLAY) p. 20

sound (SOUND) p. 5

spelled (SPELD) p. 5

tell (TEL) p. 15

wade (WAYD) p. 12

wait (WATE) p. 6

walk (WAWK) p. 4

waste (WAYST) p. 15

weigh (WAY) p. 11

weighed (WAYD) p. 13

wonder (WUHN-dur) p. 19

would (WUD) p. 20

Adjectives

An adjective describes something

alike (uh-LIKE) p. 5

clear (KLIHR) p. 18

different (DIF-ur-uhnt) p. 5

five (FIVE) p. 16

good (GUD) p. 18

her (HUR) pp. 6, 14

large (LARJ) p. 13

my (MYE) p. 7

our (OUR) p. 15

sad (SAD) p. 9

weak (WEEK) p. 17

Match these homophones to the pictures

wade
weighed

wail
whale

waist
waste

wait
weight